The Story of Mercedes Road Cars

Etienne Psaila

The Story of Mercedes Road Cars

Copyright © 2024 by Etienne Psaila. All rights reserved.

First Edition: **January 2024**

No part of this publication may be reproduced, distributed, or transmitted in any form or by any means, including photocopying, recording, or other electronic or mechanical methods, without the prior written permission of the publisher, except in the case of brief quotations embodied in critical reviews and certain other non-commercial uses permitted by copyright law.

Cover design by Etienne Psaila
Interior layout by Etienne Psaila

Website: **www.etiennepsaila.com**
Contact: **etipsaila@gmail.com**

Chapter 1: Introduction to Mercedes: Legacy of Innovation

Mercedes-Benz, a name that resonates with luxury, innovation, and unparalleled automotive excellence, has a history that dates back to the dawn of motorized travel. This book embarks on a journey through the rich legacy of this iconic brand, exploring its remarkable impact on the automotive world.

At the heart of Mercedes-Benz's story is the 1886 Patent-Motorwagen by Karl Benz, often considered the first true automobile. This pioneering invention set in motion a series of innovations that would define the automotive landscape. The fusion of Karl Benz's and Gottlieb Daimler's efforts in 1926 gave rise to the Mercedes-Benz brand, marking the beginning of a new era in automotive history. (Photo: Benz Patent-Motorwagen)

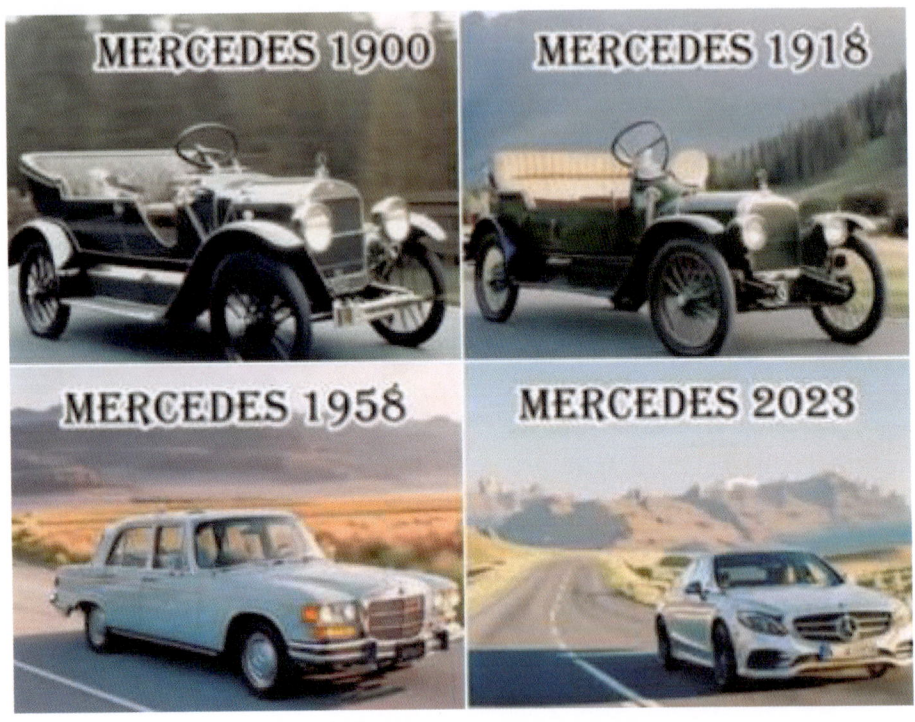

Mercedes-Benz has always been synonymous with cutting-edge technology and luxurious craftsmanship. Each model released under its banner not only encapsulates the technological advancements of its time but also reflects a persistent pursuit of perfection. From the elegant curves of the 1950s classics to the sleek, modern lines of the latest models, Mercedes-Benz cars have consistently set standards in design, performance, and comfort. (Photo: The evolution of Mercedes-Bens road cars)

The brand's commitment to innovation is not just limited to luxury and design; it extends to safety, performance, and, more recently, sustainability. Mercedes-Benz has been a pioneer in introducing features that have become standard in the automotive industry, like anti-lock braking systems and advanced driver-assistance technologies. (Photo: Mercedes's crosswind assist)

As we turn the pages of this book, we explore iconic models like the 300SL Gullwing, known for its distinctive doors and racing pedigree, and the luxurious S-Class, which has long set the benchmark for luxury sedans. We'll also delve into the revolutionary world of Mercedes-Benz electric vehicles, symbolizing the brand's commitment to a sustainable future.

Mercedes – Luxury and Elegance

This journey through the world of Mercedes-Benz is not just about cars; it's a celebration of a legacy that has continually redefined what is possible in the automotive realm. Each chapter in this book is a testament to the ingenuity, craftsmanship, and visionary spirit that Mercedes-Benz embodies, making it much more than a car manufacturer - it's a symbol of progress and excellence. Welcome to the world of Mercedes-Benz, where every model tells a story of innovation, luxury, and a relentless pursuit of perfection.

2024 Mercedes-Benz E-Class

Mercedes Maybach 2024 S680

Chapter 2: The 1954 Mercedes 300SL Gullwing: A Timeless Classic

The 1954 Mercedes 300SL Gullwing is not just a car; it's an emblem of automotive artistry and engineering brilliance. With its distinctive gullwing doors and sleek, aerodynamic design, the 300SL Gullwing captivated car enthusiasts and became a symbol of post-war automotive resurgence.

1954 Mercedes 300SL Gullwing

Born from the ashes of World War II, the 300SL was originally developed as a race car. It achieved significant success in prestigious races like the 24 Hours of Le Mans, cementing Mercedes-Benz's reputation in motorsports. The decision to produce a road version was driven by the demand for a high-performance sports car in the United States, a market rapidly growing in importance.

1956 Targa Florio – no.40 Armando Zampiero – Mario Sacchiero, Mercedes-Benz 300 SL

The Gullwing's engineering was ahead of its time. It was the first production car to feature fuel injection, which significantly boosted its 3.0-liter straight-six engine's power. This technological advancement allowed the 300SL to achieve top speeds unmatched by any other production car of its time.

What truly set the 300SL apart were its gullwing doors, a necessity born from the car's unique tubular frame which made conventional doors impossible. These doors were not just a design novelty; they were an integral part of the car's identity and allure. The interior of the Gullwing was equally impressive, combining luxury and functionality, a trait that would become a hallmark of the brand. (Photo: The 300SL's engine bay)

The car's elegant but functional interior

(Photo: Sophia Loren's Mercedes-Benz 300SL Gullwing)

The 300SL Gullwing's legacy extends beyond its technical achievements and stunning design. It marked a turning point for Mercedes-Benz, positioning the brand as a leader in the high-performance sports car segment. The Gullwing became a favorite among celebrities, further cementing its status as a symbol of sophistication and speed.

English keyboard player Jon Lord (1941-2012) from rock band Deep Purple poses with a Mercedes 300SL Gullwing coupe sports car overlooking Los Angeles, USA in June 1975

Today, the 300SL Gullwing is revered as one of the most collectible cars in the world. Its blend of beauty, performance, and innovation makes it a standout model in the history of automotive design. It is not merely a vehicle; it is a testament to the ingenuity and vision that drives Mercedes-Benz.

Chapter 3: Mercedes 600 (1963): The Epitome of Luxury

In 1963, Mercedes-Benz unveiled the 600, a car that redefined luxury and sophistication in the automotive world. This model wasn't just a vehicle; it was a statement of status, a masterpiece of engineering that catered to the elite of society.

1963 Mercedes-Benz 600 Grosser

The Mercedes 600 stood out for its imposing size, elegant lines, and an attention to detail that was unparalleled at the time. It was a blend of classic Mercedes design and innovative features that set new standards for luxury cars. Under the hood, the 600 boasted a powerful 6.3-liter V8 engine, ensuring a smooth and silent ride, befitting its distinguished clientele.

The Mercedes-Benz 600 V8 engine

Inside, the Mercedes 600 was a sanctuary of luxury. Every detail, from the rich leather upholstery to the handcrafted wood trim, was meticulously designed. It featured advanced amenities like hydraulic power-assisted controls for the windows, sunroof, and seats - a novelty at the time.
(Photo: Mercedes-Benz 600's cockpit)

Mercedes-Benz 600 Pullman's luxurious interior

The 600's list of owners reads like a who's who of the 20th century, including heads of state, celebrities, and business tycoons. This car was more than just a means of transport; it was a symbol of power and prestige. (Photo: Elvis Presley in his Mercedes-Benz 600)

Mercedes-Benz's 600 was not just about extravagant luxury; it was about making a statement. It demonstrated the brand's ability to push boundaries and create something that was so much more than a car - it was a work of art, a symbol of the highest level of automotive achievement.

Mercedes-Benz 600 - Queen Elizabeth II and the Prime Minister of Baden-Württemberg, Kurt Georg Kiesinger, on a state visit to Stuttgart in 1966 in a Pullman Landaulet

The Mercedes 600's legacy lives on as a benchmark in luxury motoring. Its influence can be seen in the luxury models that followed, both from Mercedes-Benz and other manufacturers. It remains an iconic representation of the pinnacle of luxury and exclusivity in the automotive world.

Chapter 4: Mercedes-Benz W123 (1976-1985): Durability Meets Elegance

1976 saw the debut of the Mercedes-Benz W123, a vehicle that would become a byword for durability, reliability, and understated elegance. This model carved a unique niche in the automotive landscape, becoming one of the most beloved and enduring Mercedes-Benz models ever produced.

Mercedes-Benz W123

Unlike its predecessors, the W123 wasn't designed to be the fastest or the most luxurious; instead, it focused on quality and longevity. Its build quality was exceptional, often described as 'over-engineered', a testament to Mercedes-Benz's commitment to durability. The W123's design was functional yet stylish, featuring clean lines and a balanced profile that has aged remarkably well.

Mercedes-Benz 230 E W123

The W123 series offered a range of engines, from efficient four-cylinder units to more powerful six-cylinder versions, catering to a broad spectrum of customers. These engines were known for their longevity, with many W123s clocking impressively high mileages without major issues. (Photo: The powerful and robust engine of the W123 was built to last)

Mercedes-Benz W132 Coupe, Saloon and Estate

The interior of the W123 was designed with comfort and practicality in mind. It featured high-quality materials and an ergonomic layout, ensuring a pleasant driving experience. The cabin was spacious, and the seats provided excellent support, making the W123 an ideal car for long journeys. (Photo: The W123's interior)

The W123 also marked a significant step forward in safety for Mercedes-Benz. It was one of the first cars to feature crumple zones, anti-lock brakes, and a strengthened passenger cell, reflecting the brand's commitment to passenger protection. (Photo: Comfortable seating was a part of the car's luxury)

Over its production run, the W123 gained a reputation for being a workhorse, capable of withstanding harsh conditions while offering a comfortable and refined driving experience. It became a favorite among taxi drivers, especially in Europe, further attesting to its reliability and durability.

Mercedes-Benz W123 Taxi

Today, the Mercedes-Benz W123 is celebrated as a classic, with a loyal following of enthusiasts. Its legacy is not just in its numbers, but in the stories of those who drove and loved these cars, a testament to the enduring appeal of quality and reliability over mere luxury.

The Mercedes-Benz W123's various models

Chapter 5: The 1989 Mercedes-Benz SL (R129): A Blend of Modernity and Tradition

The year 1989 marked the introduction of the Mercedes-Benz SL (R129), a car that seamlessly blended modern innovation with the timeless elegance of its predecessors. This convertible, known for its sleek design and technological advancements, set a new benchmark for luxury roadsters.

Mercedes-Benz SL (R129)

The R129 was a departure from the more conservative designs of previous SL models, featuring a more aerodynamic and contemporary look. Its design was characterized by smooth lines, an integrated rear spoiler, and a distinct wedge shape, signaling a new direction for Mercedes-Benz roadsters.

The Mercedes-Benz SL Roadster (R129)

Under the hood, the R129 boasted a range of powerful engines, including the renowned V12 in the later 600SL model. These engines provided the perfect combination of performance and refinement, befitting the SL's grand touring ethos. (Photo the R129's 7.3 liter V12 engine)

The interior of the R129 was a masterpiece of luxury and advanced technology. It featured sumptuous leather upholstery, elegant wood trim, and an array of technological features, including an automatically deploying roll-over bar for added safety during top-down driving. (Photo: The R129's beautiful interior)

The Mercedes-Benz SL R129's cabin

Safety was a key aspect of the R129's design. This model introduced innovative safety features for Mercedes-Benz, including the aforementioned roll-over bar, as well as front airbags, making it one of the safest cars of its time.

The R129 had a hydraulically-actuated automatic roll bar that would deploy if sensors detected a rollover to be imminent, deploying in three tenths of a second

The R129 was not just a car; it was a lifestyle choice, a symbol of success and sophistication. It appealed to those seeking a blend of high performance, luxury, and the unique thrill of open-top driving. (Photo: For Mercedes engineer adjusting the mirrors manually was also not safe so they developed a power mirror selection switch with three positions, left, right and middle)

The R129 has become a collectors car

Even today, the R129 is revered among enthusiasts and collectors. Its combination of style, performance, and innovative features make it a standout example of Mercedes-Benz's prowess in creating timeless vehicles.

The R129 at a Mercedes-Benz car show

The SL (R129) holds a special place in the pantheon of Mercedes-Benz models. It represents a pivotal moment where tradition met innovation, resulting in a car that was not only ahead of its time in terms of technology and safety but also one that carried the enduring elegance of the Mercedes-Benz SL legacy.

1989 Mercedes-Benz SL - R129

The R129 SL's legacy is about more than just its technical accomplishments; it's about the emotions it evokes and the memories it creates. It remains a testament to Mercedes-Benz's ability to innovate while staying true to its heritage, crafting vehicles that are not just modes of transportation but pieces of history.

Chapter 6: Mercedes-Benz S-Class (W220): Redefining the Luxury Sedan

The dawn of the new millennium saw the emergence of the Mercedes-Benz S-Class (W220), a vehicle that reimagined the concept of a luxury sedan. Introduced in 1998, the W220 brought with it a fusion of sophisticated design, cutting-edge technology, and unparalleled comfort, setting new standards in the luxury automobile segment.

Mercedes-Benz W220 S-Class

The W220 was a departure from its predecessors, showcasing a sleeker, more streamlined design. Its profile was defined by smooth lines and a more rounded appearance, moving away from the boxier look of previous models. This design choice not only enhanced its aesthetic appeal but also improved aerodynamics.

The W220 with its distinctive headlight and grille design

Inside, the W220 was a sanctuary of luxury. It offered an array of innovative features such as the COMAND system, Mercedes-Benz's cockpit management and data system, and Airmatic air suspension for an exceptionally smooth ride. The interior was a blend of hand-finished wood, fine leather, and meticulous craftsmanship, creating an ambiance of refined luxury. (Photo: The W220's COMMAND system)

1988 Mercedes-Benz S 280 (W220) interior

The W220 was not just about luxury; it was also a pioneer in automotive safety and technology. It introduced features like Distronic, the brand's first radar-based adaptive cruise control, and Pre-Safe, a system that detects an imminent collision and prepares the car and its occupants. (Photo: The Distronic cruise control)

The S-Class was the first car to be equipped with Mercedes's PRE-SAFE. PRE-SAFE more or less turns a Mercedes into a car with reflexes, as it'd be capable of reacting accordingly whenever a collision is imminent

Under the hood, the W220 offered a range of powerful engines, providing a balance between performance and efficiency. This power, combined with its air suspension and advanced chassis design, ensured that the W220 delivered a driving experience that was both dynamic and supremely comfortable. (Photo: Mercedes W220 S-Class S500 Auto - 5.0 V8)

The W220 S-Class was more than just a flagship sedan; it was a statement of Mercedes-Benz's vision for the future of luxury cars. It exemplified a perfect balance between tradition and innovation, cementing the S-Class's reputation as the quintessential luxury sedan.

Mercedes Benz S Class (W220) 6 Door Limousine

Today, the W220 is celebrated for its influence on the luxury car market, and its legacy endures in the continued excellence and innovation of the S-Class line. It remains a benchmark for luxury, comfort, and technological innovation, a testament to Mercedes-Benz's relentless pursuit of perfection in the art of car-making.

Chapter 7: The 2004 Mercedes-Benz SLR McLaren: A Fusion of Finesse and Power

2004 witnessed the birth of a legend, the Mercedes-Benz SLR McLaren. This car was not just a vehicle; it was a remarkable fusion of German engineering finesse and British racing heritage. The SLR McLaren emerged as a symbol of extreme performance wrapped in an elegantly sculpted body.

Photos: 2004 Mercedes-Benz SLR McLaren

The collaboration between Mercedes-Benz and McLaren Automotive brought together the best of both worlds: Mercedes' luxury and technological expertise and McLaren's racing DNA. The result was a supercar that stood out for its unique front-mid-engine layout, distinctive swing-wing doors, and a hand-built supercharged V8 engine.

2004 Mercedes-Benz SLR McLaren C199

The design of the SLR McLaren was heavily inspired by Mercedes-Benz's illustrious racing history, particularly the 1950s 300 SLR. Its long bonnet and distinctive gull-wing doors were a nod to this heritage, while its carbon-fiber construction was a leap into modern supercar design. (Photo: 1955 Mercedes-Benz 300 SLR)

2008 Mercedes-Benz SLR McLaren

The SLR McLaren's interior was a masterpiece of luxury, blending carbon fiber, leather, and aluminum. Despite its racing credentials, the car offered a surprisingly comfortable and luxurious cabin, making it a supercar that could be driven every day. (The SLR's beautiful interior)

Mercedes-Benz SLR McLaren 2005

In terms of performance, the SLR McLaren was nothing short of breathtaking. Its supercharged 5.4-liter V8 engine delivered extraordinary power, enabling it to accelerate from 0 to 60 mph in just over 3 seconds, with a top speed of over 200 mph. (Photo: Under the hood of the SLR)

The powerful V8 engine

The SLR McLaren also set new standards in safety for high-performance sports cars, incorporating features like ceramic brake discs and an advanced crash structure. These features ensured that the car's immense power was matched by an equally impressive level of safety. (Photo: Retention system featuring adaptive airbags, sidebags and kneebags. A cutting-edge retention system with six airbags, belt tensioners and belt force limiters completes the SLR's sophisticated safety concept, ensuring that it meets all Mercedes standard)

The Mercedes-Benz SLR McLaren remains an iconic figure in the automotive world, a testament to what can be achieved when two legendary entities collaborate. It's a vehicle that transcends its role as a supercar to become a piece of automotive art.

2009 Mercedes-Benz SLR McLaren Roadster

This chapter in Mercedes-Benz's history is not just about creating a supercar; it's about crafting a legend that perfectly encapsulates the essence of speed, luxury, and innovation - the core principles that define Mercedes-Benz and McLaren.

Mercedes Benz SLR McLaren at the Gosford Classic Car Museum

This white gold Mercedes-Benz SLR McLaren

Chapter 8: Mercedes-Benz SLS AMG (2010): Reviving a Legend with a Modern Twist

The Mercedes-Benz SLS AMG, unveiled in 2010, was a modern reinterpretation of the legendary 300SL Gullwing, a car that not only paid homage to its iconic predecessor but also pushed the boundaries of contemporary sports car design and performance.

The 300SL-inspired "Gullwing" model with a front/mid-mounted version of the brand's 6.3-litre V8 (as fitted to the majority of AMG's offerings) developing 420kW and 650Nm.

Mercedes-Benz and AMG, their high-performance division, collaborated to create the SLS AMG, making it the first Mercedes automobile to be designed and built entirely by AMG. The result was a car that embodied the spirit of the classic Gullwing while boasting state-of-the-art technology and engineering.

The design of the SLS AMG was a nod to the 1950s Gullwing, particularly evident in its long hood and distinctive gullwing doors. However, it was thoroughly modern in execution, with a lightweight aluminum spaceframe body and a contemporary, athletic stance.

The SLS AMG with its long hood and gullwing doors, drawing a visual parallel to the classic 300SL Gullwing.

The heart of the SLS AMG was its 6.2-liter naturally aspirated V8 engine, one of the most powerful at its time, delivering an exhilarating driving experience. This engine, combined with a sophisticated seven-speed dual-clutch transmission, enabled the SLS AMG to deliver both explosive performance and refined drivability.

The SLS AMG's engine, the craftsmanship and power of the 6.2-liter V8.

Inside, the SLS AMG offered a cockpit that fused luxury with functionality. The interior was a testament to Mercedes-Benz's craftsmanship, featuring high-quality materials, advanced technology, and a design that was both driver-centric and luxurious. (Photo: The SLS's interior, a fusion of luxury, comfort and technology)

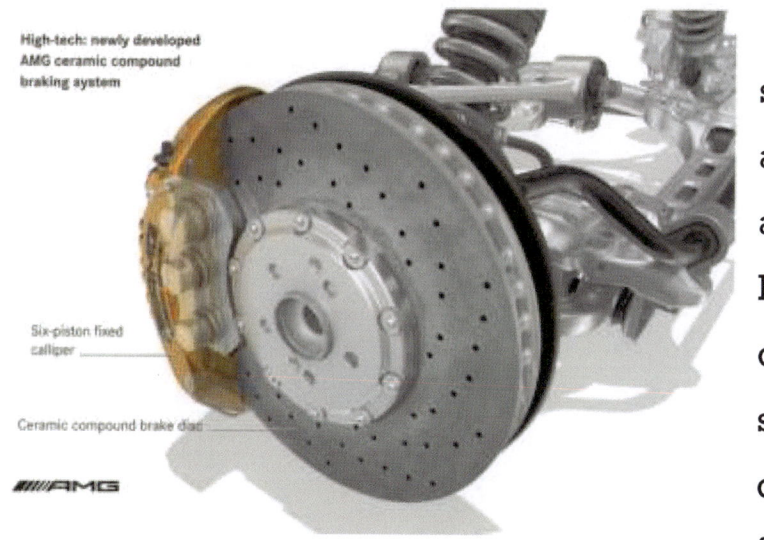

The SLS AMG also marked a significant advancement in safety and handling. It featured an adaptive suspension system, high-performance ceramic composite brakes, and sophisticated electronic stability control, ensuring that its formidable power was matched by an equally impressive level of control and safety. (Photo: The SLS's high tech braking system)

The Mercedes-Benz SLS AMG was more than just a high-performance sports car; it was a celebration of the Mercedes-Benz heritage, a modern classic that bridged the past and the future. It stood as a testament to Mercedes-Benz and AMG's ability to create a vehicle that was both a tribute to a classic and a forward-looking masterpiece. (Photo: The SLS, a tribute to Mercedes's heritage bridging the past with the future)

The legacy of the SLS AMG lies in its ability to capture the imagination just like the original Gullwing did. It remains a cherished model for enthusiasts and collectors alike, a symbol of Mercedes-Benz's enduring passion for creating cars that stir the soul and push the boundaries of what is possible.

2010 Mercedes Benz SLS AMG

Chapter 9: Mercedes-Benz A-Class (W176): Revolutionizing the Compact Segment

The launch of the Mercedes-Benz A-Class W176 in 2012 marked a significant shift in the compact car segment. This model reinvented the A-Class series, transitioning from a high-roof, MPV-styled design to a sleek, dynamic hatchback that appealed to a younger audience while maintaining the brand's hallmark luxury and innovation.

The W176 A-Class with its sleek, sporty design to appeal to a younger demographic.

Mercedes-Benz designed the W176 A-Class with the aim of attracting a new generation of Mercedes drivers. Its sporty aesthetic, characterized by sharp lines, a low roofline, and an aggressive front grille, was a radical departure from its predecessor. This bold design approach was a clear statement that Mercedes-Benz was not afraid to redefine itself and break into new markets.

The W176's distinctive front grille and sharp headlights, highlighting the car's aggressive and modern design elements.

Under the hood, the W176 A-Class offered a range of engine options, from efficient diesel models to the powerful petrol engines in the AMG variants. This range ensured that the A-Class could cater to a wide array of driving preferences, from economical city driving to performance-oriented experiences. (Photo: Mercedes-Benz AMG A 45)

The interior of the W176 A-Class was a testament to Mercedes-Benz's commitment to luxury, even in the compact segment. The cabin was a fusion of high-quality materials, innovative technology, and ergonomic design, making it both comfortable and stylish. (Photo: The W176's interior)

Safety and technological innovation were key aspects of the W176 A-Class. The model featured advanced driver-assistance systems, such as collision prevention assist and attention assist, making it one of the safest cars in its class.

The W176's 5 start NCAP safety rating

The W176 A-Class was not just a car; it was a bold statement by Mercedes-Benz, showcasing its ability to innovate and lead in new segments of the automotive market. It appealed to those seeking the prestige and quality of a Mercedes-Benz in a compact, practical form.

The W176 A-Class an appeal to modern, urban drivers.

The legacy of the W176 A-Class is found in its impact on the compact car segment and the Mercedes-Benz brand. It broadened the appeal of the brand to a wider, younger audience and set new benchmarks for what a compact luxury car could be.

The W176 A-Class represents a pivotal chapter in the Mercedes-Benz story, illustrating the brand's versatility and its commitment to appealing to a diverse range of customers without compromising on its core values of luxury, quality, and innovation.

2018 Mercedes-Benz A-Class W176

Chapter 10: Mercedes-Benz AMG GT (2014): A Symphony of Performance and Luxury

In 2014, the automotive world welcomed the Mercedes-Benz AMG GT, a model that encapsulated the pinnacle of performance and luxury. This car wasn't just a successor to the SLS AMG; it was a distinct, ground-breaking model that cemented AMG's reputation as a maker of extraordinary sports cars.

The AMG GT at full throttle

Crafted by the skilled hands at AMG, Mercedes-Benz's performance division, the AMG GT was a pure sports car with a front mid-engine configuration and rear-wheel drive. Its design was a perfect blend of elegance and aggression, featuring a long hood, a fastback rear, and dynamic proportions that spoke of its sporting pedigree.

The even more aggressive looking Mercedes-Benz AMG GT Black Series

Under the sculpted hood lay the heart of the AMG GT - a handcrafted 4.0-liter V8 biturbo engine. This powertrain was not just about raw power; it was about delivering a responsive and engaging driving experience, synonymous with the AMG philosophy. (Photo: The AMG's powerful engine)

The Mercedes-AMG GT Coupé owes its excellent performance to its performance-oriented vehicle architecture

The interior of the AMG GT was a realm of luxury. It combined race-inspired features, like the sport seats and the AMG Performance steering wheel, with high-end materials and finishes, creating an environment that was both performance-oriented and opulent. (The AMG's interior)

AMG Interior Night Package

Technologically, the AMG GT set new standards. It featured the latest in driving aids, infotainment systems, and connectivity, ensuring that it was as advanced as it was powerful. The car also boasted cutting-edge chassis and suspension technology, making it agile, precise, and exhilarating to drive.

The futuristic looking cockpit of the all new 2024 Mercedes AMG GT

The AMG GT was more than a sports car; it was a statement of Mercedes-Benz and AMG's combined expertise in creating vehicles that offer an unparalleled blend of performance, luxury, and style. It was a car that appealed to both the heart and the mind, a vehicle that was as enjoyable to drive as it was to behold.

Mercedes-AMG GT 4-Door Coupé

Today, the AMG GT continues to be revered for its combination of raw power, refined luxury, and breathtaking design. It stands as a testament to the engineering prowess and design philosophy of Mercedes-Benz and AMG, a symbol of their relentless pursuit of automotive perfection. (Photo: The 2024 AMG GT series)

The top-of-the-range Mercedes-AMG GT R exploits the full potential of the GT family and enables the impressive motorsport competence of our engineers to be experienced more intensely

The AMG GT's legacy is defined by its ability to deliver an exhilarating driving experience while enveloping its occupants in a cocoon of luxury. It remains a shining example of what can be achieved when passion for performance meets a commitment to luxury. (Photo: Mercedes-AMG GT Black Series)

Chapter 11: The Mercedes EQC (2019): Pioneering the Electric Future

2019 marked a significant milestone in Mercedes-Benz's history with the introduction of the EQC, the brand's first fully electric vehicle. The EQC symbolized Mercedes-Benz's entry into the era of electric mobility, merging their renowned luxury and innovation with sustainable technology. (Photo: Mercedes EQC)

Mercedes-Benz EQC 400 4MATIC

The EQC was a bold step for Mercedes-Benz, reflecting a commitment to an eco-friendly future without compromising on performance or luxury. Its design was both familiar and revolutionary, maintaining the Mercedes-Benz aesthetic while incorporating unique elements like the distinctive LED light strip across the front grille. (Photo: The EQC's LED light strip)

The EQC's front grille and LED lights

Beneath its stylish exterior, the EQC housed a sophisticated electric powertrain. Equipped with dual electric motors, one on each axle, the EQC offered all-wheel drive, delivering smooth, instantaneous power and exceptional performance characteristic of electric vehicles.

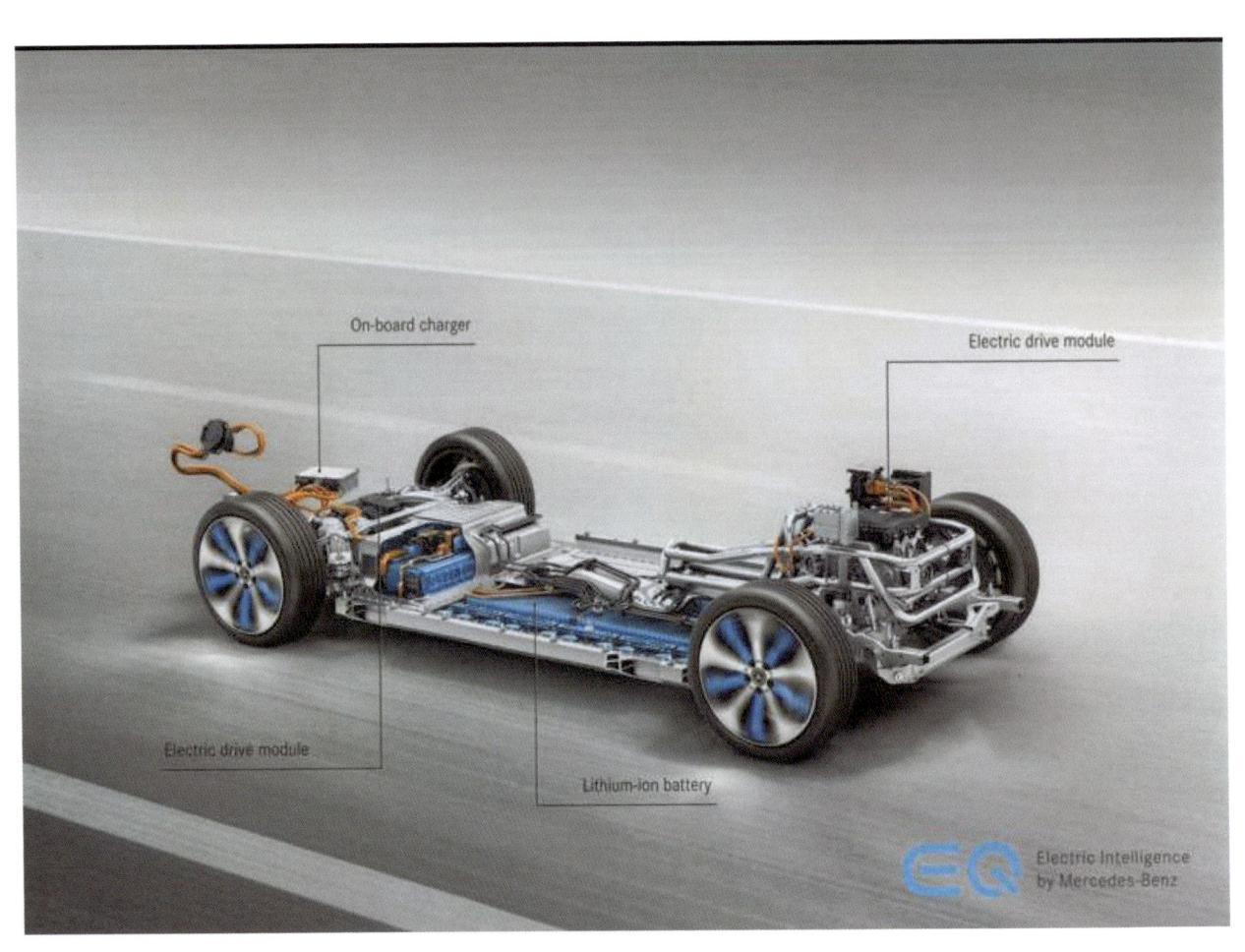

Photos: The EQC's powertrain

The interior of the EQC was a sanctuary of high-tech luxury. It featured the latest MBUX infotainment system, a widescreen cockpit, and premium materials, all crafted to create a serene and luxurious driving experience. The cabin was designed to be both elegant and functional, embracing the future of automotive interiors in an electric age. (Photo: The luxurious and technologically advanced interior)

The MBUX Augmented Reality Navigation - To enable you to find your way in complex traffic situations, MBUX Augmented Reality Navigation connects the virtual world with the real world. The technology incorporates graphical navigation instructions and traffic information into live images. You can get to your destination quickly, safely and stress-free.

In line with Mercedes-Benz's heritage, the EQC was a leader in safety and innovation. It included advanced driver assistance systems and was built on a new platform designed to protect the battery and occupants, setting new standards for safety in electric vehicles.

The EQC was not just an electric vehicle; it was a Mercedes-Benz electric vehicle. This meant that it offered the same level of refinement, comfort, and luxury that the brand was known for, now combined with the benefits of electric mobility – silent operation, zero emissions, and instant torque. (Photo: The EQC's features)

The launch of the EQC marked the beginning of a new chapter for Mercedes-Benz, one focused on sustainability and innovation. It showcased the brand's dedication to shaping the future of mobility, blending their iconic design and luxury with cutting-edge electric technology.

The EQC Symbolizes Mercedes-Benz's forward thinking approach

Today, the EQC stands as a testament to Mercedes-Benz's adaptability and vision. It represents a significant step towards a more sustainable future, proving that electric vehicles can offer the same, if not more, in terms of luxury, performance, and driving pleasure as their traditional counterparts.

The EQC is more than an electric SUV; it's a bridge to the future of the automotive industry, a beacon of Mercedes-Benz's commitment to innovation, and a promise of a cleaner, more efficient world.

The EQC is a forerunner in the brand's electric future.

Through the EQC, Mercedes-Benz has laid the groundwork for a new lineage of electric vehicles, demonstrating that luxury and sustainability can coexist seamlessly, charting a path for future innovations that will continue to redefine the automotive landscape.

Chapter 12: Mercedes-Benz S-Class (2021): The Zenith of Automotive Luxury

In 2021, Mercedes-Benz unveiled the latest iteration of its flagship sedan, the S-Class. This model was not just an update; it was a redefinition of luxury, technology, and comfort in the automotive world. The 2021 S-Class was a culmination of Mercedes-Benz's relentless pursuit of perfection.

2021 Mercedes-Benz S-Class

The design of the new S-Class blended traditional Mercedes-Benz elegance with modern sophistication. Its exterior was characterized by smooth, flowing lines, a confident front grille, and state-of-the-art Digital Light headlamps that were both functional and visually stunning.

The S-Class's Digital Light headlamps and front grille, a harmonious blend of elegance and cutting-edge technology.

Inside, the S-Class was a masterpiece of interior design. It featured a revolutionary MBUX infotainment system with a 3D driver display, augmented reality head-up display, and lush materials that included fine leather, intricate wood trim, and brushed metal accents. The attention to detail was meticulous, creating an ambiance that was both opulent and inviting. (Photo: The cockpit with its digital displays and MBUX system)

2021 Mercedes-Benz S-Class interior

The 2021 S-Class also set new benchmarks in comfort and safety. It introduced features like the rear-axle steering for improved maneuverability and the latest generation of driver assistance systems. The E-Active Body Control suspension provided an unrivaled smooth ride, adapting to road conditions in real time. The Rear-axel steering with 4.5° steering angle adjustment offers three advantages: even more superior roadholding, significantly enhanced agility and, last but not least, better maneuverability – such as when parking. The rear axle steering with 10° steering angle adjustment reduces the turning circle by almost two meters. As such the new S-

Class almost handles like a compact car when maneuvering. At higher speeds, on the other hand, you drive with the effortless superiority afforded by the long wheelbase. (Photo: Rear-axel steering)

Superior ride comfort in any situation: E-ACTIVE BODY CONTROL is a synthesis of comfort, precision and dynamism.

Performance-wise, the new S-Class was equipped with a range of powerful and efficient engines, complemented by a smooth and responsive transmission. These powertrains offered a perfect balance of power, refinement, and efficiency, befitting the sedan's status. (Photo: The powerful engine under the S-Class's hood)

The 2021 S-Class was more than a luxury sedan; it was a mobile sanctuary that combined state-of-the-art technology with timeless luxury. It catered to those who sought the ultimate in automotive comfort and sophistication.

Today, the S-Class continues to be the benchmark against which all luxury sedans are measured. It stands as a testament to Mercedes-Benz's vision and engineering prowess, a symbol of what can be achieved when passion for luxury and innovation converge. (Photo: 2021 Mercedes S-Class Raised Safety Levels for the Luxury Class)

The 2021 S-Class is not just a car; it is a statement of Mercedes-Benz's commitment to leading the way in luxury, technology, and comfort, continually pushing the boundaries of what is possible in the realm of automotive design and engineering.

Chapter 13: Mercedes-Benz EQS (2022): Sculpting the Electric Luxury Landscape

With the 2022 EQS, Mercedes-Benz sculpted a new era in luxury electric mobility. This flagship sedan did not just embody the brand's shift towards electrification; it reimagined what an electric vehicle (EV) could be, combining the luxury pedigree of the S-Class with groundbreaking electric technology.

2022 EQS

The EQS was a bold statement in design - its "one-bow" styling and cab-forward architecture represented a significant departure from traditional automotive design, optimized for electric efficiency and aesthetics. This approach resulted in a car with a drag coefficient of just 0.20, making it one of the most aerodynamic production cars ever.

2022 EQS design – a departure from traditional automotive design

Inside, the EQS offered an avant-garde cabin, featuring the revolutionary MBUX Hyperscreen - a seamless glass panel stretching the entire width of the dashboard, encompassing digital displays and infotainment functions. This futuristic approach to the interior set new standards in digital luxury. (Photo: 2022 EQS interior)

The EQS didn't just excel in aesthetics and luxury; it also pushed boundaries in electric performance and range. Equipped with a high-capacity battery, it offered an impressive range, ensuring that luxury and environmental consciousness could coexist without compromise.

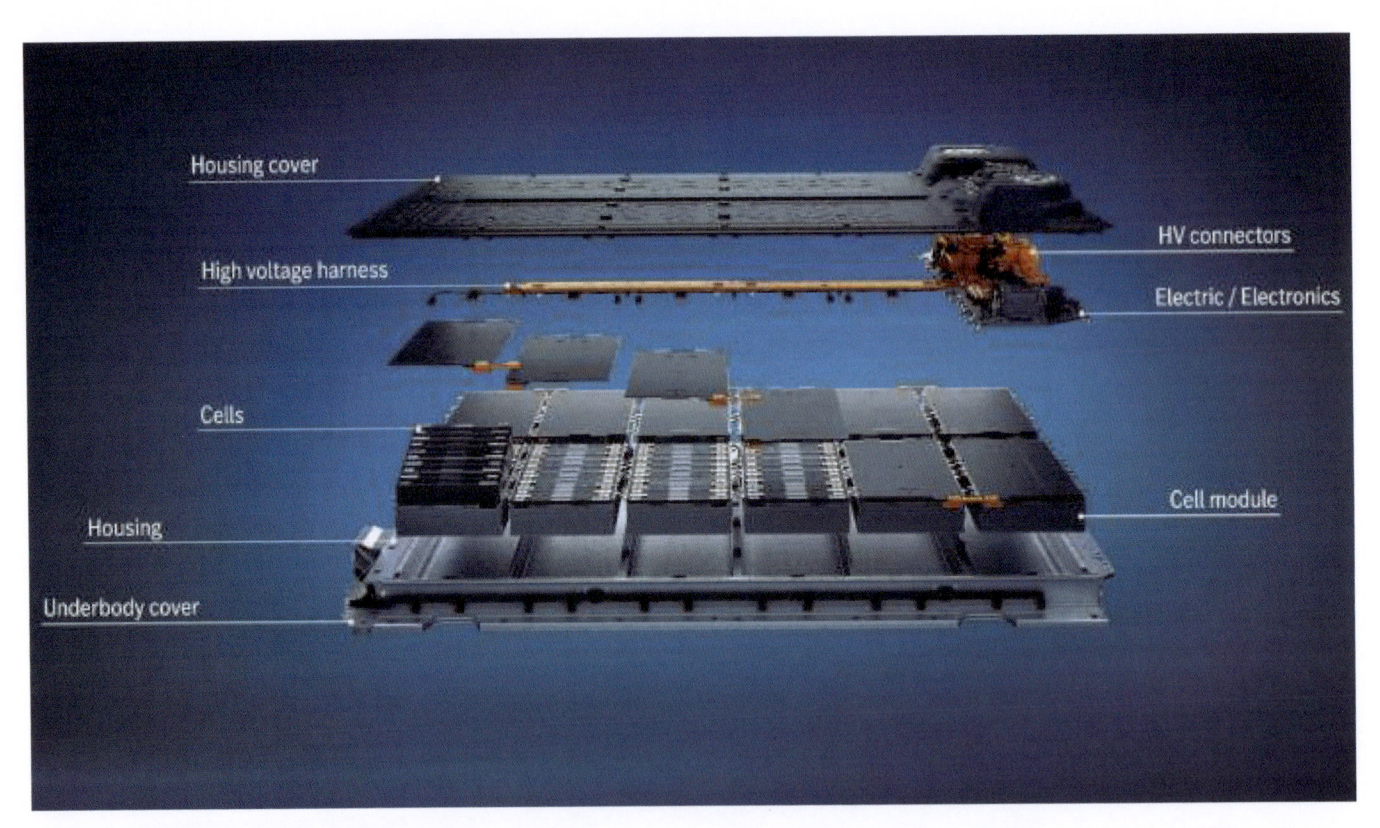

The advanced EQS battery technology - The Mercedes EQS will do 477 miles on one charge

Safety and comfort were paramount in the EQS. It included an array of advanced driver-assistance systems and pioneered new features like the HEPA filtration system, providing unparalleled cabin air quality, a reflection of Mercedes-Benz's commitment to passenger well-being.

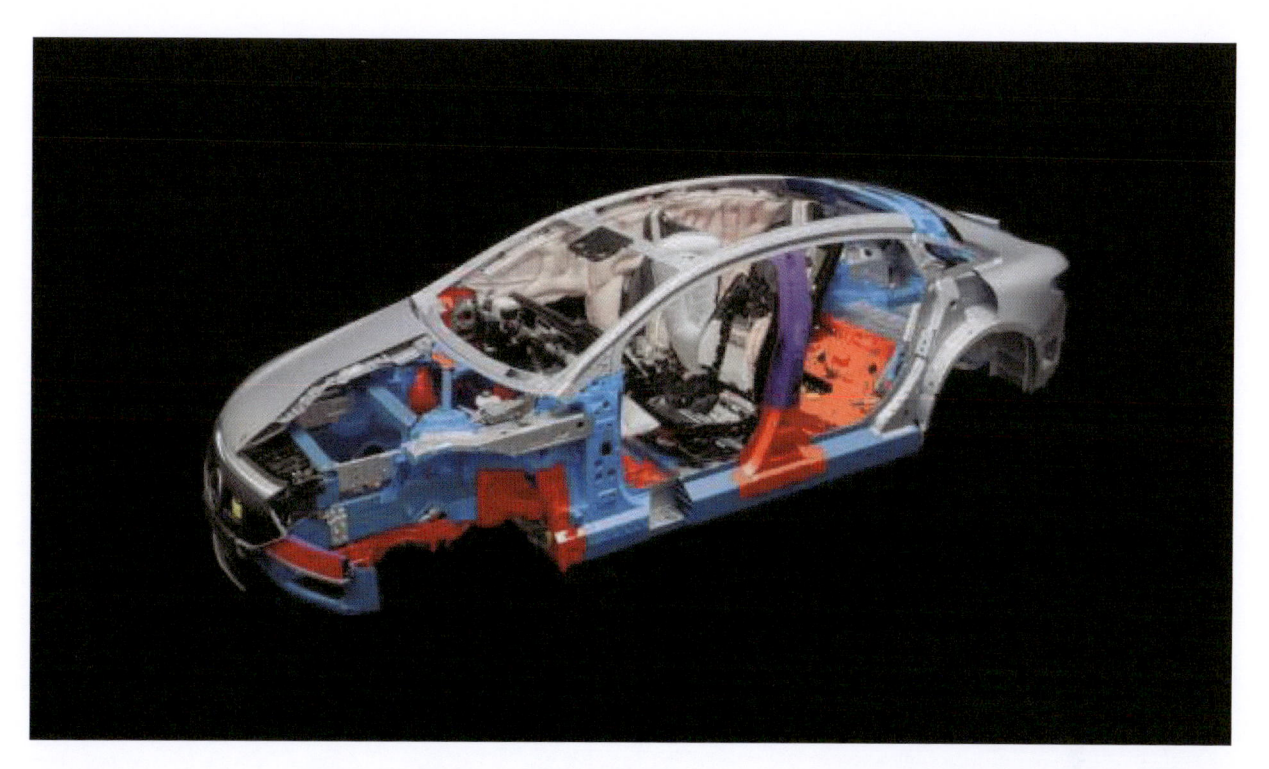

The red portions in this cutaway of the EQS denote high-strength steel while the purple represents the use of hot-formed ultra-high-strength steel.

Mercedes-Benz ensured that the driving dynamics of the EQS matched its luxurious stature. With its electric all-wheel drive and an intelligently managed power distribution system, the EQS delivered a smooth, responsive, and exhilarating driving experience, a testament to Mercedes-Benz's engineering excellence. (Photo: The EQS's futuristic and beautiful design)

The EQS was not just a car; it was a harbinger of the future, a vision of how luxury and sustainability can merge seamlessly. It demonstrated Mercedes-

Benz's ability to lead in the era of electric mobility without sacrificing the opulence and refinement that define its legacy.

"2022 Mercedes-AMG EQS First Drive: Powerful, Quiet And Refined" (Forbes Wheels)

Today, the EQS stands as a beacon in the luxury electric vehicle market, redefining expectations and setting a new benchmark for what an electric luxury car can and should be. It embodies Mercedes-Benz's ethos of 'The Best or Nothing' in the realm of electric mobility.

The EQS's legacy is not just in its technological advancements or luxurious features; it is in its ability to inspire a future where luxury and environmental responsibility coexist, paving the way for a new generation of electric vehicles that carry the prestigious Mercedes-Benz badge.

About the Author

Etienne Psaila, an accomplished author with over two decades of experience, has mastered the art of weaving words across various genres. His journey in the literary world has been marked by a diverse array of publications, demonstrating not only his versatility but also his deep understanding of different thematic landscapes. However, it's in the realm of automotive literature that Etienne truly combines his passions, seamlessly blending his enthusiasm for cars with his innate storytelling abilities.

Specializing in automotive and motorcycle books, Etienne brings to life the world of automobiles through his eloquent prose and an array of stunning, high-quality color photographs. His works are a tribute to the industry, capturing its evolution, technological advancements, and the sheer beauty of vehicles in a manner that is both informative and visually captivating.

A proud alumnus of the University of Malta, Etienne's academic background lays a solid foundation for his meticulous research and factual accuracy. His education has not only enriched his writing but has also fueled his career as a dedicated teacher. In the classroom, just as in his writing, Etienne strives to inspire, inform, and ignite a passion for learning.

As a teacher, Etienne harnesses his experience in writing to engage and educate, bringing the same level of dedication and excellence to his students as he does to his readers. His dual role as an educator and author makes him uniquely positioned to understand and convey complex concepts with clarity and ease, whether in the classroom or through the pages of his books.

Through his literary works, Etienne Psaila continues to leave an indelible mark on the world of automotive literature, captivating car enthusiasts and readers alike with his insightful perspectives and compelling narratives.
He can be contacted personally on **etipsaila@gmail.com**